SUMMARY:

STEVE JOBS

ABBEY BEATHAN

Text Copyright © Abbey Beathan

Legal & Disclaimer

Legal & Disclaimer

The information contained in this book is not designed to replace or take the place of any form of medicine or professional medical advice. The information in this book has been provided for educational and entertainment purposes only.

The information contained in this book has been compiled from sources deemed reliable, and it is accurate to the best of the Author's knowledge; however, the Author cannot guarantee its accuracy and validity and cannot be held liable for any errors or omissions. Changes are periodically made to this book. You must consult your doctor or get professional medical advice before using any of the suggested remedies, techniques, or information in this book. Images used in this book are not the same as of that of the actual book. This is a totally separate and different entity from that of the original book titled: "Steve Jobs".

Upon using the information contained in this book, you agree to hold harmless the Author from and against any damages, costs, and expenses, including any legal fees potentially resulting from the application of any of the information provided by this guide. This disclaimer applies to any damages or injury caused by the use and application, whether directly or indirectly, of any advice or information presented, whether for breach of contract, tort, negligence, personal injury, criminal intent, or under any other cause of action.

You agree to accept all risks of using the information presented inside this book. You need to consult a professional medical practitioner in order to ensure you are both able and healthy enough to participate in this program.

Table of Contents

The Book at a Glance

This book sheds light on the interesting life of Apple Inc. co-founder Steve Jobs.

Here's what to expect in each chapter:

Chapter One recounts Steve Job's childhood from the time that he was adopted by Paul and Clara until he became seriously interested in electronics.

Chapter Two talks about the first time he met Stephen Wozniak who later on became a significant figure in terms of the success of Apple.

Chapter Three narrates how Steve had started to become a rebellious son. Paul and Clara were already having a difficult time raising him but, nonetheless, they continued to support him and show unconditional love.

Chapter Four focuses on the employment of Steve at Atari and his increasing interest in spirituality and Zen Buddhism, which eventually led him to a vacation in India.

Chapter Five narrates the birth of the Apple I personal computer, and how it inspired Steve to establish a business called Apple Computer.

Chapter Six recounts the incorporation of the business, which he and his business partners registered as Apple Computer Co. This eventually led to the birth of Apple II, an increase in manpower, as well as an increase in the company's credit line. This chapter also narrates the negative behaviour displayed by Steve, which was increasingly becoming an issue among his co-workers.

Chapter Seven focuses on Steve's personal life in which he got Chrisann Brennan pregnant. He also had to face court charges to make him provide child support.

Chapter Eight talks about the failure of Apple III, the creation of Project Lisa, and Steve's disruptive behaviour that led to a reorganization that he was not informed of.

Chapter Nine focuses on the decision of Apple co-founders to go public which made Steve, Wozniak, and Mike Markkula millionaires. During this time, Steve had also started to be featured in magazines.

Chapter Ten recounts the birth of Project Macintosh that was initially led by Jef Raskin but was eventually – and controversially – transferred to Steve.

Chapter Eleven mainly focuses on the personality of Steve as a leader and how, despite his disruptive behaviour, he nonetheless managed to make the employees stay motivated.

Chapter Twelve recounts how the design of Macintosh came to be one step at a time.

Chapter Thirteen offers information on Steve's skill of motivating his team through his inspirational talk. In spite of his offensive behavior, his team had learned to work effectively with him.

Chapter Fourteen talks about the decision of Mike Markkula to step down as Apple's interim president. He was replaced by John Sculley, who was then the president of Pepsi-Cola.

Chapter Fifteen describes the efforts done by Steve to make the first ad of Macintosh a successful one.

Chapter Sixteen offers information on the professional relationship between Bill Gates and Steve. Often described as "frenemies," they both had unimaginable passion for business and technology, yet, they differed in so many ways.

Chapter Seventeen talks about the ouster of Steve from Apple brought about by his antithetical behaviour.

Chapter Eighteen focuses Steve's establishment of and the difficulties he faced with his NeXT computer business following his ouster from Apple.

Chapter Nineteen narrates Steve's major investment in Pixar and the start of its success in digital animation.

Chapter Twenty relates Steve's opportunity to meet his biological mother, Joanne, and his full sister, Mona, and how both women became part of Steve's real family.

Chapter Twenty-One talks about his personal relationship with Laurene Powell whom he eventually married and had children with.

Chapter Twenty-Two speaks of the advent of Pixar's success when it released its computer-generated film "Toy Story," which became the top-grossing movie of the year in 1996.

Chapter Twenty-Three offers information on the move made by Apple to acquire Steve's NeXt business.

Chapter Twenty-Four narrates the decision of Apple to offer the CEO position to Steve, which he did not accept. Nonetheless, he was able to help the company seal a deal with Microsoft.

Chapter Twenty-Five talks about the efforts done by Steve to come up with Apple's second ad. In this chapter, Steve also became the company's interim CEO.

Chapter Twenty-Six offers information on how Steve and Jony Ive successfully collaborated to come up with designs for Apple products.

Chapter Twenty-Seven talks about the enormous success of the iMac, which was introduced as a home consumer product in 1998.

Chapter Twenty-Eight relates the decision of Steve finally to agree to become Apple's chief executive officer.

Chapter Twenty-Nine focuses on the plans of Steve to come up with Apple retail stores.

Chapter Thirty talks about Steve's vision of creating a digital hub wherein a single gadget would be used to access text messages, photos, and music, among many others.

Chapter Thirty-One offers information on the advent of the iTunes Store, and how it bothered Microsoft.

Chapter Thirty-Two focuses on the songs uploaded in Steve's iPod, including all the songs of Bob Dylan and the Beatles.

Chapter Thirty-Three talks about the challenges faced by Steve and Pixar when DreamWorks released its animated film "Antz" to compete with Pixar's "A Bug's Life."

Chapter Thirty-Four relates the launching of the G4 Cube personal computer in 2000. It was during this time when Steve was contemplating about releasing a flat screen iMac.

Chapter Thirty-Five narrates the time when Steve was diagnosed with cancer. In spite of his illness, he continued to work as Apple's CEO.

Chapter Thirty-Six talks about the advent of the iPhone, and how Steve envisioned the creation of the iPad tablet.

Chapter Thirty-Seven offers information on the deteriorating health condition of Steve. Nonetheless, he was there to launch personally the iPhone 3G in 2008.

Chapter Thirty-Eight focuses on the official launching by Steve of the iPad in 2010.

Chapter Thirty-Nine talks about the challenges that Apple faced in terms of the Android operating system released by Google, the refusal of Adobe to develop a type of software for Apple, and the flaw discovered in iPhone 4.

Chapter Forty narrates the difficulties faced by Steve caused by his cancer. Nonetheless, he was able to launch the iPad 2 and be updated of the movies being created by Pixar in 2011.

Chapter Forty-One relates the worsening health condition of Steve and his decision to resign from Apple.

Chapter Forty-Two finally talks about Steve's legacy.

Introduction

How This Book Came to Be

Steve Jobs and the author have known each other since 1984, as Jobs would always contact the latter to cover product launches. However, when the author left his work at CNN and Time Magazine, they lost communication. It was only in 2004 when he heard from him again as Jobs contacted him and requested to write a book about his life.

The author has been known for publishing biographies of notable and influential people including Albert Einstein and Benjamin Franklin. When Jobs expressed his interest in getting his life story published, the author suggested postponing such plan until his retirement. Several times, Jobs would always talk him into writing his biography. At times, the author would even find Jobs' persistence puzzling until his wife told him that Jobs contacted her and told her about his cancer. The author then knew that he indeed had to write Jobs' biography.

Jobs told him about his interest in both humanities and electronics. He told him of how he looked up to businessmen Bill Hewlett and David Packard. They were Jobs' inspiration for establishing – and later on, achieving – his ultimate goal of creating a business that would outlive him.

Jobs gave the author all the liberty to write about him. He even encouraged people –including those he had aggravated and offended – to talk and help in gathering all information needed to finish the book. Even Jobs' wife did not order any limitations at all. In fact, she strongly urged the author to discuss in detail all of her husband's failures and successes.

While writing this biography, the author learned so many things about Jobs' personal and professional life. His unbelievable passion and grit allowed him to succeed in six different industries including digital publishing, tablet computing, phones, music, animated films, and personal computers.

In this book, you will learn how Jobs' life as an adopted child gave him the opportunity to maximize his talents and become a worldwide success.

CHAPTER ONE

CHILDHOOD

Abandoned and Chosen

A boy was born to Joanne Schieble and Abdulfattah Jandali on February 24, 1955.

Unfortunately, Schieble and Jandali could not raise their newly-born son because Schieble's strict Catholic family strongly disapproved of her relationship with a Muslim. They had no choice other than to put their son up for adoption.

Schieble was not very particular of the personality and the profession of the family that would adopt her son. However, she strictly required the adoptive parents to be college graduates. Initially, her son was supposed to be adopted by an attorney and his wife, but the couple backed out last minute and informed Schieble of their decision to instead adopt a girl. In the end, her son was ironically adopted by a high school dropout named Paul Jobs and his wife named Clara Hagopian. They then named their adopted son Steven Paul "Steve" Jobs.

When the adoption case was closed, it took them twenty years to finally see each other again.

Paul and Clara never hid from Steve the fact that he was adopted. It was never an issue to Steve too because Paul and Clara made sure that he always felt well loved. In fact, he described Paul and Clara as his real parents.

Paul's passion included mechanics and automotive. That's why, as a child, Steve was exposed to these things, and Paul never failed to impress Steve every time they hang out with each other in the garage of their house in Silicon Valley, California. Through Paul's passion, Steve also became exposed to electronics – and that was what seriously caught Steve's interest.

As Steve was growing up, he sensed that he was smarter than his parents. He soon became aware too that his parents knew of this fact, and that they were definitely aware that he was not like any other average child. They noticed his extraordinary intelligence and, because of that, they always made sure that Steve would have the chance to study in better schools. They always expressed their one hundred percent support for Steve.

In spite of being intelligent, Steve was not doing well in school during his younger years. He was bored and always ended up getting into trouble. Nonetheless, his parents never got mad at him. In fact, his father would even blame the school for not being able to motivate him.

Until one day, his fourth grade teacher Imogene Hill challenged him to work on math problems in exchange of a lollipop and five U.S. dollars. This ignited Steve's desire to learn more and it gave his teachers the realization that he was indeed intellectually special. The teachers then suggested Steve to skip fifth and sixth grades, and instead attend the seventh grade in the next school year to prevent him from getting bored and to maintain or improve his enthusiasm about studying. Paul then agreed to allow Steve to skip fifth grade only.

Paul had always been supportive of Steve. He would even drive him to attend the Hewlett-Packard (HP) Explorers Club where children were urged to build anything. In the case of Steve, his first project was to create a frequency counter.

One fateful day, while he was trying to finish his frequency counter, he realized that he lacked some parts. His solution? He called Bill Hewlett, HP's chief executive officer, and told him about his dilemma. Indeed, he did not only get the parts that he needed, but he also landed a job at HP.

This was the beginning of his serious passion for electronics.

CHAPTER TWO

ODD COUPLE

The Two Steves

When Steve was in high school and a student of electronics teacher John McCollum, he met and eventually became friends with Stephen "Woz" Wozniak. At that time, Woz was already a graduate and was five years older than Steve.

Because of Woz's vast knowledge of electronics, Steve learned a whole lot from him. Woz was also amazed of Steve's passion for electronics and his eagerness to learn more. However, more than anything else, Woz was in awe of Steve's leadership and business skills.

Together, they launched their very first product in 1971 called the Blue Box, which was a device that offered free long-distance telephone calls. Initially, they created it to do prank calls such as calling the Vatican to pretend that Woz was political scientist Henry Kissinger wanting to talk to the pope. Until, one day, Steve realized that the Blue Box could be more than just a device for fun as he seriously thought of selling it.

Therefore, the two Steves worked on producing one hundred Blue Box devices. One device cost them forty U.S. dollars to build and they offered it for one hundred fifty U.S. dollars per device to interested buyers. Surprisingly, they were able to sell almost all of their stock.

The Blue Box business had made Steve and Woz realize that they could indeed have a future in the electronics business. The income that Blue Box generated gave them tremendous confidence to continue their business partnership and eventually to create new electronic products. With Steve's exceptional business vision combined with Woz's prodigious engineering skills, the two Steves could smell future success.

Once, in an interview with Steve, he expressed his belief that Apple Inc. would not come into fruition had it not been because of the Blue Box device.

CHAPTER THREE

THE DROPOUT

Turn On, Tune In...

In 1972, before he graduated from senior high school, he began dating Chrisann Brennan who was a junior high school student at that time.

Chrisann described Steve as crazy and fun to be with, which made her attracted to him. Steve was sometimes rude and cold at her but they had too many similarities that made them a strange but fun combination. Steve loved playing the guitar and writing poetry while Chrisann loved drawing and painting.

After Steve's graduation in the same year, Steve announced to Paul and Clara his intention to live in a cabin above Los Altos, California with Chrisann. Apparently, his parents strongly disapproved of him doing so, but he was adamant of his decision.

Despite Steve's hardheadedness, Paul and Clara nonetheless continued to show their support towards him. One time, Steve's car caught on fire and Paul drove all the way to his location to rescue him.

After his graduation from high school, Steve somewhat considered not going to college anymore. However, his parents talked him into obtaining a college education in accordance with a pledge they made in relation to his adoption – that Paul and Clara had no choice other than enroll him in college. Steve then chose Reed College in Oregon.

At Reed College, Steve learned about meditation and the League for Spiritual Discovery (LSD). He began reading books about spirituality including, but not limited to "Be Here Now," by Baba Ram Dass, "Cutting Through Spiritual Materialism," by Chogyam Trungpa, and "Zen Mind, Beginner's Mind," by Shunryu Suzuki.

Aside from spirituality, meditation, and Zen Buddhism, Steve became serious about vegetarianism as well. In fact, he began reading books about it too. In general, these things all formed part of his college life. He hardly indulged in electronics during that time.

However, as time passed by, Steve found himself getting bored of college life. He decided to drop out of college because he felt guilty that his parents' hard-earned money was just going to waste. He then decided just to take up classes that were of interest to him such as calligraphy – which explains the existence of the different typefaces in the Apple Mac.

CHAPTER FOUR

ATARI AND INDIA

Zen and the Art of Game Design

After leaving Reed College in 1974, Steve found a job at Atari as a technician. Because of his arrogance, many did not like him but Atari founder Nolan Bushnell admired his intelligence. Soon, Steve was helping Atari enhance the video game designs.

One of the main reasons why Steve wanted to work was to save money so he could go to India to continue his spiritual journey. One time, he told Atari chief engineer Al Alcorn about his plan, including his intention to borrow money from him for his travel expenses. Al and Steve then came to an agreement that Steve would first fly to Europe to fix an interference problem encountered by Atari there. Once done with such assignment, Steve would fly directly to India from Europe.

Steve stayed in India for seven months. There, he learned how to use his intuition. He once said that in the United States, Americans always use their intellect, while in India, the strength of the people is their intuition. During his stay in

India, Steve was able to develop his skill of using intuition, and he believed that such skill had a magnificent effect on his career.

When he came back to the United States, Steve still continued his quest for self-awareness and personal growth. He also confided to some of his friends that his quest was primarily related to the fact that he was adopted.

Aside from his continued soul-searching, he also went back working for Atari. In 1975, Nolan gave Steve an opportunity to develop a new version of the Pong video game. Steve then asked Woz to help him work on it, and whatever the amount that Steve would earn from that project, he would split the amount to pay Woz.

Woz and Steve forced themselves to finish their project within four days because Steve told Woz that they strictly had four days to finish everything. The truth is, Nolan did not specify any kind of deadline that was all Jobs' idea. This made Nolan and everyone else at Atari, including Steve, realize that Steve indeed had skills not only in engineering, but in business too.

CHAPTER FIVE

THE APPLE I

Turn On, Boot Up, Jack In...

In the '70s, computing was starting to become a symbol of liberation and individualism. Technology was surprisingly being embraced by the counterculture, and as explained by musician Bono, it was because people of the counterculture and those who embraced technology saw things differently.

Portola Institute was a foundation that supported computer education, and the People's Computer Company was one of the organizations that Portola helped launch. People's Computer Company was merely a newsletter and a group with members that met on a weekly basis to discuss personal electronics.

In the January 1975 issue of the publication "Popular Mechanics," the People's Computer Company members saw on its cover the very first Altair personal computer kit. When they had the privilege to have an Altair kit in the office, group members Fred Moore and Gordon French decided to launch the first ever meeting of the Homebrew Computer Club. One of the attendees was Woz.

Right after that very meeting, Woz was conceptualizing in his mind and on paper what a personal computer should look like. Each day and night, Woz worked hard to develop a type of software that would display images on the computer screen, until he made that happen on June 29, 1975.

Steve was amazed when he learned about it, as he then started accompanying Woz to club meetings. When Woz expressed his intention to produce a computer that he would donate to others, Steve disapproved of it. Woz recalled that Steve could always find a way to make money out of his designs. They knew that they already needed to establish a computer company – which, of course, became known as Apple Computer.

The first personal computer created by Woz was, of course, named Apple I.

CHAPTER SIX

THE APPLE II

Dawn of a New Age

In 1976, Woz was already working on the prototype of Apple II. The aim was to launch a complete package of personal computer – a fully integrated product starting from the computer software down to the power supply, with a built-in keyboard, and an attractive case. To make this happen, Steve coordinated with different people with different expertise. Along the way, Steve and Woz met Mike Markkula, a retiree at thirty-two years old who previously worked for Intel and Fairchild Semiconductor.

After coming up with a business plan, Mike then was urged to invest a maximum of US$250,000 – but with conditions. First, Mike insisted that the business be incorporated and, second, that he be made an equity participant. In January 1977, Apple Computer then became Apple Computer Co.

It was during this time when Apple hired art director Rob Janoff to create a new logo. This was the birth of the apple with a bite featuring six psychedelic colors in stripes.

The Apple II was launched at the West Coast Computer Faire in San Francisco, California in April 1977. At that event, three hundred orders of the Apple II were made. Moreover, Steve had the opportunity to meet Mizushima Satoshi, a textile manufacturer who became the first dealer of Apple computers in Japan.

After the success of the Apple II, their business finally started to look like a real company. They had a credit line, employees, and daily work pressures. From the garage of Steve's parents, Apple Computer Co. moved to a rented office in Cupertino. Moreover, for the next sixteen years, the Apple II was marketed in different models with approximately six million units sold.

However, as time passed by, Steve was growing to be more and more temperamental and authoritarian. Moreover, his hygiene was becoming more and more of an issue as well. But because Mike and Woz were both disinclined to confrontations, Mike decided to hire Mike "Scotty" Scott as the new president of Apple. His job was mainly to control Steve.

During this time, Steve was also conceptualizing a new product that he could call his masterpiece because, in spite of the success of Apple II, the credit was mainly given to Woz.

15

CHAPTER SEVEN

CHRISANN AND LISA

He Who Is Abandoned...

In spite of Steve's and Chrisann's on-off relationship, Steve got Chrisann pregnant, and on May 17, 1978, Chrisann gave birth to Lisa Nicole Brennan.

The child did not use Steve's surname because, at that time, Steve seemed disconnected from his personal life. In fact, he even doubted if he was the father of Lisa until he took a DNA test to confirm. The result indicated that he was indeed the father – 94.41%. Nonetheless, he managed to say that there was still a huge probability that Lisa was not her daughter. Through the California courts, however, Steve signed an agreement acknowledging his role as the father, was ordered to provide child support, and was instructed to pay the county for the back welfare payments provided to Chrisann.

In an interview held decades after the birth of Lisa, Steve expressed his regret for doubting that Lisa was her child. He expressed regret for not being able to take care of Chrisann during her pregnancy and for not being able to take care of both of them as Lisa was growing up. What Steve knew at that time was that he was not ready to marry and become a father, which explained why he was totally disconnected from reality. In spite of being able to provide financially for Chrisann and Lisa following the court case, Steve nonetheless knew that he could have at least done better as Lisa's father.

After the court case, they all moved on with their lives. Chrisann focused on raising Lisa while Steve focused on his job. He stopped taking drugs, minimized his time doing Zen Buddhism, and was not a strict vegan anymore.

It was also during this time when Steve began dating Barbara Jasinski.

CHAPTER EIGHT

XEROX AND LISA

Graphical User Interfaces

There was no denying that the Apple II was a huge success, but Steve knew that it would last forever. He also knew that in spite of the ideas he incorporated to make the Apple II way better than the Apple I, it would always be regarded as Woz's masterpiece. He seriously wanted to launch his own product that would make a mark. He wanted a product that would become his legacy.

He thought his legacy would be the Apple III as it had better features than Apple II. It could handle both lowercase and uppercase letters and could display more than forty characters. It also had a larger memory. It was in 1980 when Apple III was launched. Unfortunately, it was a failure. Steve then moved forward, thinking of a new product to build. The company then hired engineers who conceived a machine featuring a sixteen-bit microprocessor. The machine was called LISA, which meant Local Integrated Systems Architecture. However, in reality, the machine was intentionally named after Steve's daughter.

During this time, Apple employee Jef Raskin opened up an opportunity for the company to enter the premises of the Palo Alto Research Center (PARC) of Xerox Corp. Steve also allowed Xerox to invest in Apple for as long as Apple would be given the opportunity to learn about the technology that Xerox was working on at that time. Indeed, it was at the Xerox PARC where Apple realized the future of computing.

All the plans of Apple were promising and everyone was willing to work hard for it. However, Steve's disruptive behavior was increasingly becoming a concern among his co-workers. This led to a reorganization that Steve knew nothing about. In other words, Steve was stripped off any operations control.

CHAPTER NINE

GOING PUBLIC

A Man of Wealth and Fame

In 1980, business partners Mike, Woz, and Steve decided to go public through Apple's initial public offering. By the end of the year, the company was valued at 1.79 billion U.S. dollars.

There were employees who got shares of stock and one of them was Rod Holt, the engineer who was in charge of the power supply of the Apple products. Daniel Kottke, however, was not given a single share of stock in spite of being with Apple from the time that they were still all working in Steve's garage. Aside from that, Daniel played an important role in the personal life of Steve. He was there during Steve's spiritual journey and during the pregnancy of Chrisann. He, in fact, even allowed Steve and Chrisann to share a rental house with him. Technically, Daniel and Steve were best friends. Nonetheless, Steve didn't give him stock options.

Woz, on the other hand, was extremely generous as he shared his wealth with other Apple employees. He only made sure that he purchased his dream house. The rest of his shares were then sold to other employees at a discount. He also gave shares to other Apple workers whom he believed had been shortchanged.

Steve did not share his stocks with anyone. That's why at the age of twenty-five, his net worth totaled to 256 million U.S. dollars.

He then began to do philanthropic activities. However, the largest personal gift he ever gave was the US$750,000-worth of stocks for his parents. It gave Paul and Carla the opportunity to pay off their mortgage and allowed them to go on cruises at an annual basis. Other than that, Paul and Carla did not splurge on anything else. They continued to live a simple life.

These scenarios tell us that Steve's attitude towards wealth varied as he was both selfish and generous in some ways. Nevertheless, when he did not share his stocks with other Apple employees the way Woz did, it did earn him recognition. He became the cover boy of several magazines including, but not limited to, "Inc." and "Time." He started to be known worldwide as a young millionaire.

CHAPTER TEN

THE MAC IS BORN

You Say You Want a Revolution

Jef Raskin was hired by Apple in 1976 when Steve was looking for someone who could write the Apple II manual. From then on, Jef became the company's Publications Department Manager.

However, Jef's ultimate dream was to build an affordable personal computer for every individual. He talked Mike into it until, and then in 1979, Jef was given the opportunity to work on that small project – which Mike named the Macintosh.

Steve was removed from Project Lisa, and so when he learned about Project Macintosh, he was extremely curious about it. Apple officers anticipated the conflict that transpired between Jef and Steve, but since Scotty removed Steve from Project Lisa, he felt it was fair to let Steve work on Project Macintosh this time. Anyway, it was considered a minor development project only and was housed in a different building.

Jef, who was then asked to take a leave of absence from Apple, eventually found work at Canon where he continued the project that he had in mind. His finished product was the Canon Cat machine.

Meanwhile, what Steve had in mind for Macintosh was to create a compact version of the Lisa machine. He successfully took over the Mac division and began hiring people to complete his team.

During this time, Scotty seemed to be losing his leadership skills and the top managers all agreed that it was high time that he'd be replaced. Markkula then took over as the interim president. This paved way for Steve to have full control of the Mac division.

CHAPTER ELEVEN

THE REALITY DISTORTION FIELD

Playing by His Own Set of Rules

Apple employees, especially those who worked in the Macintosh division, had different stories to share about the attitude and behavior of Steve Jobs. The common description, however, was that it was difficult to work under Jobs. They used the term "reality distortion field," a term derived from Star Trek, to describe his charisma.

One of the employees, Debi Coleman, stated that the Macintosh division got entangled in Steve's reality distortion field. It was as if they were being brainwashed by their leader. It was difficult to work with him, but there's no denying that his attitude was what led the team to work hard and to make the impossible possible.

Ann Bowers, Apple's human resource manager at that time, could say that she somehow had the power to calm Steve down whenever he had one of his tantrums. She was like a mother figure to Steve. There were times when he would visit her and her husband at home for dinner. In fact, it seemed as if Steve had treated them as his surrogate family.

Steve was a big source of daily work stress and to make things light in the Macintosh division, the employees came up with an "annual award ceremony" for the person who successfully stood up to him for one entire year. For consecutive years, it was Joanna Hoffman who got the award. Her skill of standing up to him led to her promotion as head of manufacturing.

Nonetheless, no matter how others perceived Steve's behavior as negative, they do admit the fact that he had helped them become better people one way or another. They did not only improve their skills, but they had become mentally and emotionally stronger too. Steve was a significant figure in terms of their personal and professional growth.

CHAPTER TWELVE

THE DESIGN

Real Artists Simplify

As a child, Steve grew up listening to his father talk about automobiles. There were times when Paul would emphasize the positive impact of automotive design on consumers. That's why Steve knew from the very start that exquisite industrial design would make Apple exceedingly stand out from other electronic companies.

Beginning in 1980, Steve had been researching on industrial design, and he's been thoroughly thinking of what designs should be incorporated to Apple products.

One time, Steve asked Bill Atkinson if they could come up with dialogue boxes and other windows with rounded corners. Bill did not see its importance so he argued with Steve but, in the end, Steve won the argument, of course.

Then, Steve wanted to come up with as many variations of typefaces as possible, so they hired Susan Kare to focus on this area. Apple engineer Andy Hertzfeld and Susan initially named the fonts after Philadelphia cities. Steve did not like this and asked that they'd be changed and named after world-class cities such as London, San Francisco, and New York.

Steve learned from Mike how presentation and packaging mattered to consumers. That's why he hired the services of German designer Hartmut Esslinger, who then suggested to Steve that the Apple products should feature thin grooves, rounded curves and white cases.

It was from his father that Steve learned about ensuring that all aspects of a product should be beautifully done, even those hidden ones. He then exerted his effort to improve how the printed circuit board looked like.

He gathered his Macintosh team one time and asked them all to sign their names on a drafting paper, which were then etched inside each Macintosh. Apple users may not know it but everyone from the Macintosh team knew right from the start that their signatures were all inside each device.

CHAPTER THIRTEEN

BUILDING THE MAC

The Journey Is the Reward

While Steve was building the Macintosh personal computer, he made sure that he was aware of the products of the competitors such as the IBM PC. In spite of the success of IBM, Steve was not intimidated by it. However, he did not only regard other companies as competitors, he also regarded Lisa as a competitor of Macintosh.

While building the Mac, he intentionally made it incompatible with Apple II and Lisa. This came as a concern among Apple employees as Steve seemed to be destroying not only Lisa but Apple as a whole through his soon-to-be released Mac computer.

Steve incorporated several limitations to the features of Mac. One of these was to ensure that the case would be different from other personal computers available in the market – so hackers, hobbyists, and repairmen could not easily open them and tinker with the insides. Pretty much a reflection of Steve's controlling personality, the Mac apparently offered users a controlled experience.

In 1982, Steve was highly confident of the features of Mac that he immensely expected to be declared by "Time" Magazine as its Man of the Year. To his dismay, this did not happen. Instead, the Mac personal computer was particularly chosen by "Time" to be featured as its 1982 Machine of the Year.

In January 1983, Apple launched the Lisa, which, unfortunately, was a flop. With Steve as Apple's spokesperson, it seemed as if he intentionally did what he could to make Lisa fail. During the launching, Steve mentioned the plans of Apple to launch Macintosh as a cheaper version of Lisa. As anticipated, consumers chose not to buy the Lisa and instead wait for the launching of Macintosh.

The death of Lisa left Apple without any choice but with hope that Macintosh would be a success. This also meant that Apple had heavily to depend on Steve's project.

In spite of the obnoxious behavior of Steve, he also knew how to lift up the spirit of his team. In fact, he would even take them on retreats on a bi-annual basis where he would always deliver an inspirational talk. As time passed by, the Mac team learned to stand up to Steve.

CHAPTER FOURTEEN

ENTER SCULLEY

The Pepsi Challenge

When Scotty left Apple, Mike temporarily replaced him as company president, but Apple did not seem to exert an effort to look for a permanent president anymore. However, when Mike's wife ordered him finally to find his replacement, he and Steve started their quest for their new leader. Among all their prospects, it was John Sculley whom they, specifically Steve, liked the best.

John was the president of Pepsi-Cola before he was hired by Apple to become its president. Mike and Steve intentionally decided not to hire a technology executive, but instead hire someone with expertise in consumer marketing and advertising, a description that perfectly fit John.

Instantly, John liked Steve and vice-versa. They admired each other's intelligence. According to John, he could see his younger self in Steve.

During John's first few days as Apple's president, he seemed to encounter culture shock daily. He had a lot of trouble adjusting to the casual environment of Apple. He was used to wearing formal business clothes at Pepsi-Cola, but at Apple, he had to dress down. He was used to a formal corporate meeting setup but, this time, he had to get used to Steve sitting on the floor during meetings. John always tried to follow a meeting agenda, but it always ended up as debates and complaints of various topics.

In spite of the similarities between John and Steve, they also clashed. In addition, one of the conflicts that transpired between them was John's insistence that the Mac be sold at a price higher than what Steve had in mind.

CHAPTER FIFTEEN

THE LAUNCH

A Dent in the Universe

The very first ad for the Macintosh was aired at the Super Bowl XVIII, which announced that it would be launched on January 24, 1984. The ad, which was aired only once, had such an impact it was chosen by Advertising Age and TV Guide as the best advertisement of all time.

Indeed, Steve had always known how it was to get the attention of journalists and consumers.

There was a time when Jobs tasked Apple's technology writer Steven Levy to feature the Macintosh team on the cover of the "Rolling Stone" magazine. It was something that Steven felt was impossible. True enough, his story about the Macintosh team failed to make it to the magazine cover. At that time, it was frustrating. But as years passed by, Steven witnessed how every story he wrote featuring Steve always ended up on the cover of world-renowned magazines such as "Business Week," "Newsweek," and "Time."

Finally, on January 24, 1984, the Macintosh was launched at

the Flint Auditorium of De Anza Community College to coincide with Apple's annual stockholders' meeting. Instead of Steve doing all the talking, he allowed the Mac to speak for itself. It was the very first personal computer that introduced itself. The Mac received a standing ovation.

Each Macintosh team member received a commemorative Macintosh computer with a plaque, which was personally handed to each one of them by Steve.

Jef, Woz, and John must admit that, in spite of the rough management style of Steve, nobody else could pull off Mac's creation the way Steve could.

CHAPTER SIXTEEN

GATES AND JOBS

When Orbits Intersect

During the development of Macintosh, Jobs would often talk to Bill Gates, the principal founder of Microsoft Corp., to help him with the Macintosh operating system.

In spite of the similarities between Steve and Bill in terms of their interest in business and technology, their personalities totally differed. Bill focused on computer coding and analytic processing power whereas Steve focused on making a delightfully designed device user-friendly. Bill was interested in selling Microsoft operating system and software licenses to manufacturers while Steve was inclined to integrating content, software and hardware in one package.

Steve and Bill's relationship was something that could be termed as "frenemy." There were times they would be at each other's throats, but there were also times that they seemed to be the best of buddies. Bill was basically part of the Macintosh crew. In fact, he was present in all the bi-annual retreats that Jobs set up.

Bill once described Steve as someone who was not very knowledgeable of technology. Nonetheless, he had that unbelievable instinct of what would and would not work.

One of the incidents that infuriated Steve was when Bill launched the Microsoft Windows operating system. Jobs accused Gates of cloning the Macintosh, but Gates then explained that he took inspiration from the machine exhibited at Xerox PARC -- pretty much like how Apple was inspired to create Macintosh when it saw the same machine.

Many believed that Windows was not as elegant as the Macintosh interface. Nonetheless, Windows improved and eventually dominated the operating system sector.

CHAPTER SEVENTEEN

ICARUS

What Goes Up...

Following the successful launch of Macintosh in 1984, John decided to assign both the Lisa and the Macintosh divisions to Steve. This decision did not seem to turn out well as Steve promoted Macintosh team members while one-fourth of the Lisa team were laid off.

In the second half of the year, Macintosh sales started to decline due to low quality while Lisa sales were totally nonexistent because it was costly. Because there was still quite a lot of stock of Lisa machines, Steve decided to launch the Lisas as a new product, which he then called the Macintosh XL. Joanna Hoffman felt it was fraud so she decided to resign.

Members of the Macintosh Team began to resign one by one including Andy Hertzfeld, Burrell Smith, and Bruce Horn, among others. Among all those who left the company, it was the resignation of Woz that came as a big surprise. Woz had always been in charge of Apple II and, at the time of his resignation, it was still the company's largest selling product.

Unfortunately, it seemed as if his efforts were not being appreciated and Steve gave very little attention to the Apple II division.

Steve and John always had a good professional relationship. However, as time passed by, the complaints against Steve increasingly worsened. His behavior wildly fluctuated. John also knew that Steve would sometimes say negative things about him.

John decided to ask Steve to leave the company as Apple was already starting to have an unhealthy work environment because of him. However, Steve did not give up easily. He plotted something to oust John as president, but, unfortunately for Jobs, John and the rest of the top management found out about this plan, and so, during a board meeting, all the directors voted for the ouster of Steve.

CHAPTER EIGHTEEN

NeXT

Prometheus Unbound

After his ouster from Apple, Steve decided to establish his own business. This, however, led to legal disputes against Apple due to several reasons such as allegedly luring away several Apple employees and allegedly establishing a business intentionally to compete with Apple, among others.

Nonetheless, he continued to establish his business, which he called NeXT. He started coming up with a logo, his business card, an industrial design, and all other things by contacting the suppliers whom he met through Apple.

However, Steve did not find it easy to deal with them and he knew that in order to make things easier, he needed to resolve the legal case that Apple had filed against him. Steve was, in fact, fortunate that John and all other Apple directors were willing to reach an out-of-court agreement. As how Paul Rand put it, Jobs just needed to learn some lessons.

Therefore, Steve continued working on his NeXT computer.

He did not only personally shell out a big amount of money, but he was able to lure other investors as well.

The NeXT Team found it difficult to manufacture and engineer the NeXT computer all because of Steve's perfectionism. The casing alone, which cost more than US$600,000, was difficult to produce and had to be created separately. With regard to the operating system, he tried to talk Bill Gates into creating one specifically for NeXT, but Bill refused to do so. Apparently, Bill was one of the people that Steve could not easily lure.

It was in 1989 when the NeXT computer started to be on sale and the expectation was that the sales would be approximately ten thousand units on a monthly basis. Unfortunately, they were only making sales of approximately four hundred units per month.

CHAPTER NINETEEN

PIXAR

Technology Meets Art

It was in 1985 when Steve had the opportunity to meet Ed Catmull through Alan Kay, an Apple fellow who used to work for Xerox PARC. Ed was in charge of the computer division of Lucasfilm Ltd, a company founded by film director George Lucas. At that time, Lucas needed a buyer for the division and, coincidentally, Steve was willing to buy it. Steve's passion for hardware, software, and computer graphics were the factors that inspired him to invest in it. The most significant piece of hardware that the division had at that time was the Pixar Image Computer, and so, they decided to use Pixar as the name of the new company.

Originally, Pixar's digital animation business was only a sideline. It was mainly established as an avenue to showcase the company's software and hardware. In other words, the digital animation business mainly formed part of Pixar's marketing strategy.

At the 1986 SIGGRAPH annual computer graphics conference, Pixar exhibited a short animated film titled Luxo

Jr. Soon, it had an Academy Award nomination and Steve even flew to Los Angeles, California to attend the ceremony. Luxo Jr. did not win, but Steve ultimately saw the huge potential of Pixar to succeed in the digital animation business.

He then asked his Pixar family to create a computer animated full-length film. However, while it was being created, Pixar was starting to lose money. Steve had to make sure that his Pixar investment would not go to waste – not after being ousted at Apple and with all the problems encountered at NeXT. Pixar then created "Tin Toy" which won the Academy Award for best animated short film in 1988.

Shortly thereafter, Pixar started to get an offer to establish a production deal with Disney.

CHAPTER TWENTY

A REGULAR GUY

Love Is Just a Four-Letter Word

In spite of devoting most of his time to business, Steve also always had time for his family. When his adoptive mother, Clara, got stricken with lung cancer, Steve spent most of his time with her. He also found time to exert an effort to look for his biological parents. However, he only contacted his biological mother, Joanne Schieble, after Clara passed away in 1986, as he did not in any way wanted her adoptive parents to get offended. For Steve, Paul and Clara would always be considered his real parents. After Clara died, Steve asked for Paul's consent to contact Joanne – to which Paul open-mindedly agreed to.

Steve then finally visited Joanne at her house in Los Angeles, California. He learned that she had been divorced from his biological father for a long time already. He also learned about her full sister, Mona Simpson, who at that time was living in Manhattan, New York and was working as a novelist. Joanne then contacted Mona and arranged for Steve's meeting with her.

Steve was euphoric to have met Mona as they had a lot of similarities. In a short span of time, they became close friends. Steve even once said that he was not at all expecting himself to develop such closeness to Mona, mainly because he was never close to her adopted sister, Patty. It never entered his mind that he would someday be close to a sibling.

Soon thereafter, Joanne and Mona eventually became part of his real family as the two ladies would regularly spend Christmas season at Steve's house. Steve had always been honest about not being interested to meet his biological father, Abdulfattah Jandali, and it was not because of the fact that Jandali abandoned him. More than anything else, it was because of the fact that Jandali abandoned Joanne and Mona.

Steve's opportunity to be reunited with Joanne and Mona paved the way to improve his relationship with his own biological daughter, Lisa Brennan. Steve began visiting her as often as possible. He started bringing her to his office and he even brought her with him during an out-of-the-country business trip.

Steve was also in and out of several intimate relationships. Among the ladies that entered his life were Joan Baez, Jennifer Egan, and Tina Redse.

CHAPTER TWENTY-ONE

FAMILY MAN

At Home with the Jobs Clan

After Steve's breakup with Tina in 1989, he met Laurene Powell.

One fateful day, Laurene formed part of the audience when Steve delivered a talk titled "View from the Top" at the Stanford Graduate School of Business. Laurene had no intention of attending Steve's lecture and was merely dragged along by her classmate. That was why no more seats were available when she entered the room – which became a blessing in disguise as she was then asked to sit right in front of the stage, and right next to where Jobs sat before the lecture started.

Steve was enamored by Laurene's beauty, and so, after Steve's lecture, he immediately invited her out to dinner – to which Laurene agreed to. They were inseparable since then.

In December 1990, Laurene got pregnant with Jobs' second child. However, unlike Steve's decision when he got Chrisann pregnant, he intended to marry Laurene. On March 18, 1991, Steve and Laurene got married.

Soon thereafter, Lisa moved in with Laurene and Steve. Steve was definitely exerting his effort to improve his relationship with Lisa but because of his inconsistency – he would sometimes act sweet and would all of a sudden turn cold, there were also times when they would not speak to each other.

A few months following Steve's marriage to Laurene, Reed Paul Jobs was born. The married couple had two more beautiful children named Erin Siena and Eve. Just like how Lisa felt, Erin and Eve somehow had a distant relationship with their father – as he would sometimes be a sweet father to them and all of a sudden would turn into a cold person. However, his relationship with his son, Reed, was strong.

CHAPTER TWENTY-TWO

TOY STORY

Buzz and Woody to the Rescue

There were numerous debates between Jobs and Jeffrey Katzenberg, head of the film division of Walt Disney Co., before they finally agreed to establish a partnership in May 1991. Their very first project was the animated film titled "Toy Story."

It took the Pixar-Disney team years to finish "Toy Story", mainly because of technical concerns. During the first months, there were numerous disagreements and disapprovals transpiring, particularly when it came to the story itself and its production. Steve chose not to meddle in terms of the creative process. He was, however, the guy to depend on in terms of coordinating with Disney and when it came to cost control. Jeffrey had always been amazed of Steve's capability to control the budget efficiently.

In November 1995, "Toy Story" premiered at the El Capitan Theater in Los Angeles, California. Being a film that came into fruition due to a Disney-Pixar partnership, the Pixar team was, of course, expected to attend the event. However, when Steve felt that the premiere night made it seem like the film was solely a Disney production, he decided not to attend. Instead, he organized a premiere event of his own at the Regency theater the following day. He himself delivered the speech to launch the film. These two premieres apparently confused people as to whether "Toy Story" was a Pixar or a Disney film. But it wasn't such a big deal anyway, especially when the film began its regular screening – with a bang.

"Toy Story" earned thirty million U.S. dollars during its first weekend – and it was for domestic screening alone. Following the last day of screening, the film generated a total of over three hundred sixty million U.S. dollars internationally. This apparently made "Toy Story" the top-grossing movie of the year and it defeated such movies as "Apollo 13" and "Batman Forever."

After such success, Steve knew that Pixar had to generate more income, and so he thought of an initial public offering.

CHAPTER TWENTY-THREE

THE SECOND COMING

What Rough Beast, Its Hour Come Round at Last…

Hardware had always been Steve's passion, but as NeXT's income was declining, he knew he had to give up manufacturing hardware. Instead, he focused on offering operating system licenses to machine manufacturers. The business nature of NeXT became pretty much similar to that of Microsoft – it's just that Microsoft was dominating the industry and NeXT was definitely not.

Such move was similar to what transpired at Pixar when he had to give up producing Pixar hardware and instead focus on computer animation. In spite of his disappointments that were brought about by NeXT, he was nonetheless doing fine focusing his time on his family and the booming Pixar business.

However, he still found himself thinking a lot about the personal computer industry. He was not happy with how Apple was turning out to after his ouster. He believed that

Microsoft replicated the graphical user interface of the Macintosh and introduced its own version to the market until it finally dominated the desktop computer industry with tremendous success. During that time, Apple was not introducing any new product at all.

Also during this time, John Scully remarked about the intention of Steve – before his ouster – to make Apple a consumer products company. John could not perceive what Steve could envision. What John knew at that time was that high-technology products could not be offered as a consumer product.

As Bill Gates described all that subsequently transpired, it was all a twist of fate. Apple acquired NeXT despite the fact that NeXT was not doing that well. Following that acquisition, the NeXT operating system was not used by Apple at all. The advantage of such an acquisition, however, was that Apple was able to bring in Avie Tevanian to the company as he had the capability immensely to improve the Apple operating system.

Another advantage was that Apple had brought back Steve to the company, which perhaps at that time was a big nightmare to Apple employees, but he turned out to be the company's greatest   CEO.

CHAPTER TWENTY-FOUR

THE RESTORATION

The Loser Now Will Be Later to Win

Apparently, it was Steve's strategy to lure Apple into acquiring NeXT so he could make a comeback. As soon as he turned forty in 1995, things unfolded the way he perceived them to be – "Toy Story" was a massive success, he re-joined Apple, and he was out there to prove that even people in their forties have innovative minds. He was out there to prove that he could not only improve the capabilities of the personal computer, but he could provide consumers with ultimate experience in terms of listening to music, reading books, using mobile phones, and watching movies, among many others.

Gil Amelio was the company's chief executive officer when Steve rejoined the company as an advisor. During Gil's tenure, he was faced with various corporate problems such as an unruly corporate culture, a weak business strategy, low-quality products, and declining income, among others. Amidst all those issues, he was being bad-mouthed by Steve.

In the second quarter of 1997, the stock performance of Apple dropped due to an anonymous sale of over a million shares of stock – only to find out that it was Steve who sold his shares. As unfortunate events transpired one after another, Gil started to have a strong inkling that Steve was apparently manipulating his termination.

In one of the most crucial board meetings, Apple director Ed Woolard informed the other directors of his analysis of the company's future. He explained that Apple was nearing bankruptcy and it seemed like Gil had no capacity to save the company, whereas with Steve, there was a bigger chance that Apple could survive.

When Steve was offered the CEO position, he declined. Nonetheless, the directors continued to oust Gil.

Steve continued working for Apple as an advisor. However, as anticipated, he acted like its CEO as he was involved in various areas of the business including advertising, supplier negotiations, cost control measures, and product design, among many others.

Everyone at Apple, including the directors, allowed him to do what he wanted to do. One of his first accomplishments when he made a comeback was sealing a deal with Microsoft.

CHAPTER TWENTY-FIVE

THINK DIFFERENT

Jobs as iCEO

In July 1997, Steve contacted Lee Clow, the creative director responsible for Apple's "1984" ad that was shown during a Superbowl game. Steve wanted Lee to create a new ad for Apple – thus, the birth of the slogan "Think Different."

On a weekly basis, Steve made sure that he would be in a three-hour meeting with his preferred advertising agency, as well as his marketing and communications teams. He would always tour them to the company's design studio and would passionately explain to them all the developments.

In September 1997, Steve finally accepted the position of CEO but his commitment to his position was tentative. In fact, he did not sign any contract and he did not take any salary. This prompted him to be referred to as the iCEO – wherein the "i" could mean interim or indefinite. Besides, he could not officially take the position as he was the CEO of Pixar at that time.

During this time, Bill Gates was extending his help to make

Apple a lucrative business. He was suggesting Apple officers to offer the Macintosh operating system to other personal computer manufacturers. Unfortunately, Steve was not in favor of it.

Steve instructed Apple employees to do product review presentations for him to come up with potential products that they could release in the future. Most, if not all of these presentations led to termination and lay-offs.

Steve may oftentimes be harsh but he always knew what he was doing. In this case, one of the most important things that he had taught the Apple team was the importance of "focus."

CHAPTER TWENTY-SIX

DESIGN PRINCIPLES

The Studio of Jobs and Ive

Jony Ive was the head of the design team of Apple. In spite of the well-known rough behavior of Apple's iCEO, Steve and Jony had gotten along well.

Steve described Jony as a very intelligent person. He particularly liked Jony because of his capability to understand marketing and business concepts. For Steve, Jony was not only a designer. Jony had both macro and micromanagement skills. He highly understood what kind of company Apple was. In simpler terms, Steve and Jony seemed always to have the same wavelength.

They both believed in the importance of design to making a product sellable. If most companies believe that design should be driven by engineering, Steve and Jony believed otherwise. For them, especially for Steve, design should come first and the engineers had to find a way to make all components fit inside.

CHAPTER TWENTY-SEVEN

THE iMAC

Hello (Again)

The iMac desktop computer was the very first Apple product that achieved success under the collaboration of Steve and Jony. Launched in 1998, the iMac's target market was home consumers.

While coming up with the iMac design, Jony and Danny Coster, his top deputy, presented several futuristic designs to Steve. As anticipated, approximately a dozen designs were rejected. The good thing about Jony's professional relationship with Steve, Jony always thoroughly considered Steve's ideas and he always accepted Steve's criticisms – and vice versa.

Steve emphasized that he wanted a curvy and playful looking computer to entice home consumers. When Jony and Danny refined their design for the last time, they got a hundred percent approval from Steve.

During the launching of iMac in Cupertino, Steve decided to invite former Apple executives Mike Scott and Mike

Markkula, and the original members of the Mac division. When Steve unveiled the new product, he remarkably gained the approval of the audience.

In August 1998, the iMac, which was in bondi blue color, was released in the market. By December 1998, it was recognized as the fastest-selling computer in the history of Apple. Soon thereafter, Jony and Danny came up with iMacs in other interesting colors, which made the iMac even more sellable.

In the midst of iMac's success, Steve was already thinking of a new product to release – he was seriously contemplating about focusing on the music market this time.

CHAPTER TWENTY-EIGHT

CEO

Still Crazy after All These Years

The success of iMac further reaffirmed what others already knew about him even from the time that he co-founded Apple with Woz – that he was indeed a visionary and a creative person.

"Focus" had always been his management mantra, and he always believed in the saying "Simplicity is the ultimate sophistication," which originated from Leonardo Da Vinci and popularized by Steve. He previously used such quote as a slogan for his Macintosh ad campaign. He also applied such adage in the internal operations of Apple, emphasizing that simplicity could only be achieved by, first, overcoming complexities.

Steve stopped manufacturing products in Apple factories and started outsourcing everything – from raw materials to the finished product. This meant even the suppliers had to face the meticulous discipline imposed by Steve.

There were Apple officers and staff who still could not bear

Steve's behavior and some even quit, including the company's head of operations. While the company was in search of their new head of operations, Steve was the one overseeing the department. This occurred for almost a year until he met Tim Cook. Steve and Tim had similarities in terms of running a company, which made Steve instantly like him. Tim was previously a Compaq Computers manager focusing on procurement and supply chain until Steve hired him as head of operations. He became a significant part of Apple as he efficiently addressed issues related to operations and the production process.

During this time, Steve met fashion designer Issey Miyake who made his black turtlenecks, which eventually became Steve's signature style. At Apple, Steve developed a culture of collaboration. If other companies believed in putting limitations on the schedule of their meetings to allow employees to become more productive, Steve believed in as many meetings as possible. He also banned slide presentations during meetings as he preferred his employees hashing out issues and offering their ideas in an informal manner.

Apple officers and staff had always been aware of how gifted Steve was in terms of having an eye for talent. Finally, in 2000, Steve agreed to leave his iCEO position to become Apple's chief executive officer.

CHAPTER TWENTY-NINE

APPLE STORES

Genius Bars and Siena Sandstone

Steve aimed to achieve triumph in terms of innovation and he believed that it would only be possible by finding a strategy to improve communication to clients. His solution was to develop several Apple retail stores.

Steve wanted the Apple stores to be situated in malls to bring convenience to its customers. He wanted it to be minimalist. He wanted Apple to offer few products only to avoid confusion among customers, and he wanted the retail store to have ample space so customers would find it comfortable to try out the different Apple products.

There were companies that experienced financial loss when they opened suburban stores. That's why when Steve presented to the board of directors his idea of opening up retail stores, the directors were not elated. However, Steve was still able to convince them to approve a trial run of four retail stores.

While there were several directors who most of the time did

not agree of Steve's ideas, Millard Drexler was particularly different as he supported Steve's plans for the company. Steve liked him too. Steve looked up to him because of his big accomplishment – as Gap CEO, Millard was able to successfully transform Gap from an ordinary clothing store into a famous brand of casual culture in the United States.

Apple's first retail store opened in May 2001 and was a colossal success. Indeed, Steve's ideas had given a further boost on how brand image and retailing were perceived by people.

The most successful Apple store of all was the one along Fifth Avenue in Manhattan, New York. It attracted approximately fifty thousand visitors per week, on the average, in its first year of operations in 2006.

CHAPTER THIRTY

THE DIGITAL HUB

From iTunes to the iPod

In 2001, Steve knew that Apple had to offer something new, and so, he thought of coming up with a personal computer that would serve as a "digital hub." Meaning, the computer user would be able to access his text messages, videos, photos, music, and other digital files using a single device.

The "digital hub" idea was conceived in 1990s and it was 1999 when Apple started developing a type of software where art and technology would go hand in hand. Such application software now includes iTunes, GarageBand, iPhoto, iDVD, and iMovie, among others.

Steve was correct to realize that music would gain more popularity in 2000 as he incorporated the CD burner as one of the iMac's features. However, he knew that it wasn't enough. He wanted iMac users to be able to effortlessly transfer and manage music using their computers and then eventually burn their own playlists – thus, the birth of iTunes.

Steve, who had always been passionate about music, then

envisioned the probable success of introducing a portable music player. He collaborated with several geniuses in the field of design and engineering, such as Jon Rubinstein and Phil Schiller, for the development of this new product – thus, the birth of iPod.

It was apparent that the products being launched during the tenure of Steve were one by one becoming a massive success.

CHAPTER THIRTY-ONE

THE iTUNES STORE

I'm the Pied Piper

The advent of the iPod portable music player and the iTunes software were perhaps two of the reasons why the music industry began to face a challenge. In order to use the iPod, a user had to purchase a CD to copy the songs to the iPod, or the user could download music online, which would also then be transferred to the iPod. While piracy may have been present even before Apple came into existence, nonetheless, iPod and iTunes opened up a room for consumers to patronize piracy services. Several illegal websites became available wherein consumers could download music for free. This resulted in a decline in the legal sales of CDs in 2002. Steve knew that he needed to address this issue to allow iPod and iTunes users to download music on a legal, safe, and simple manner. This led to the development of the iTunes Store, where users could purchase a single song or an entire album.

Steve collaborated with several record companies and other computer-related businesses to make the iTunes Store a success. Moreover, on April 28, 2003, Steve launched it at the Moscone Center in San Francisco, California.

With the iTunes Store, everyone benefitted – and still benefits – from it. Users and Apple itself are not the only ones that benefit from it – even the artists and record companies also do.

Somehow, the success achieved by iTunes Store bothered Bill Gates. Bill knew that he and his team also had to find a strategy to maintain their competitiveness in the market. Bill, however, did not deny the fact that Steve indeed made an amazing job of getting the approval of music companies to collaborate with him.

CHAPTER THIRTY-TWO

MUSIC MAN

The Sound Track of His Life

The success of the iPod phenomenon was unbelievable. It came to a point wherein the standard question that iPod users asked one another was, "What's on your iPod?" In fact, even notable public figures – whether artists, athletes, or politicians – were asked this question during interviews.

As Steven Levy, author of the book "The Perfect Thing," put it, the iPod did not simply had songs that the owner liked, it was a product that could actually describe the personality of the owner.

Steve's iPod contained all the songs by Bob Dylan and the Beatles. Steve, being a Beatles and Dylan fan, downloaded all the albums in its entirety. The rest of the music on his iPod were not complete albums but were, nonetheless, songs of his other favorite artists such as Simon and Garfunkel, Jimi Hendrix, the Doors, and The Monkees, among many others. Even when iPod became obsolete and in the advent of the iPad, Steve made sure that the contents of his iPod were all transferred to his new gadget.

Being a die-hard Dylan fan, Steve decided to offer a digital "boxed set" of Dylan's songs on the iTunes Store. At first, Dylan's record label was not in favor of it but Steve always had the power to talk people into something he badly wanted to do. So, in August 2006, Dylan's digital boxed set was launched on the iTunes Store. In return, Dylan agreed to appear in an iPod TV ad.

Aside from Dylan and the Beatles, Bono of U2 was also Steve's favorite. They also had the opportunity to sign a co-branding deal.

CHAPTER THIRTY-THREE

PIXAR'S FRIENDS

... and Foes

The second computer-animated film made by Pixar was "A Bug's Life," which faced challenges prior to its release in 1998. Steve and the rest of the Pixar team had a conflict with DreamWorks SKG as the latter wanted to intentionally release its own computer-animated film "Antz" – simultaneously with "A Bug's Life."

In the end, "Antz" was released several weeks earlier than "A Bug's Life," and earned almost two hundred million U.S. dollars worldwide. "A Bug's Life" then earned almost four hundred million U.S. dollars worldwide.

"Toy Story 2" was then released in 1999, which earned the biggest among the three Pixar computer-animated films released by far, with almost five hundred million U.S. dollars ticket sales worldwide. The success of the three films ultimately resulted in Steve's firm decision finally to construct a showcase headquarters for Pixar.

In 2002, conflict arose between Steve and The Walt Disney

Co. CEO Michael Eisner. This was resolved when the Disney board of directors decided to oust Eisner and replace him with Bob Iger, the chief operating officer of Disney.

During this time, the iPod was only capable of handling music and videos. Therefore, Steve and Bob collaborated to come up with an Apple gadget that would allow users to watch television shows.

CHAPTER THIRTY-FOUR

TWENTY-FIRST-CENTURY MACS

Setting Apple Apart

Following the successful launch of the iMac, Steve and Jony agreed and ensured that the succeeding Apple products would all have a signature design. Apple products needed to stand out from the rest to make them saleable amidst the global success of Windows.

In 2000, Apple released the G4 Cube personal computer. The uniqueness of its design allowed it to end up on display at the Museum of Modern Art in New York. However, it was not a success because of its high-end features. Professionals were simply not enticed to have a jewel-like sculpture in their workstations. Unfortunately, Windows was still the choice among workaday professionals.

Nevertheless, this occurrence did not discouraged Steve from coming up with new designs. Steve always knew how to move forward, and it was one positive trait that he possessed. Therefore, he and Jony soon thereafter contemplated on releasing a new version of iMac – this time, with a flat-screen monitor.

During this time, Steve also collaborated with other excellent players in the computer industry such as Intel and Motorola to upgrade the capabilities of the iMac. Such capability of Steve to collaborate with different companies to make Apple products competitive in the market was a skill that Bill Gates truly admired of him.

CHAPTER THIRTY-FIVE

ROUND ONE

Memento Mori

It was in 2003 when Steve was diagnosed with cancer. He later on speculated that his cancer could have resulted from the stress he experienced beginning 1997 when he was running both Pixar and Apple. In fact, during that time, Steve developed several illnesses including kidney stones.

When he learned about his cancer, he informed some of his colleagues about it. At that time, he preferred to treat himself using natural medication such as acupuncture, hydrotherapy, and juice fasts, among many others. His family and colleagues had been encouraging him to undergo surgery but Steve simply did not want to. Finally, in 2004, Steve agreed to undergo surgery.

However, during his healing process following the surgery, Steve needed to eat fish, meat, and other full-fat milk products to ensure that his body would get enough protein. However, because of his obsessive diets that only included fruits and vegetables, Steve never had proper food consumption that could have been significant to his recovery.

71

Unfortunately, the doctors discovered several liver metastases that led to chemotherapy treatments. This, however, made him face more challenges in terms of his diet.

Steve then kept quiet about his continuing fight with cancer. After his chemotherapy, he was telling everyone that he had been healed.

While Steve was on medical leave, he was temporarily replaced by Tim Cook. When Steve came back, he was amazed by the way Tim had run the company while he was away. This prompted Steve to make Tim Apple's chief operating officer in 2005.

CHAPTER THIRTY-SIX

THE iPHONE

Three Revolutionary Products in One

The sales of iPod were spectacularly increasing. In fact, in 2005 alone, approximately twenty million units were sold. During that time, Steve was already thinking of coming up with a gadget that could incorporate the features of the iPod into that of a smartphone. Again, he contacted several key players in the technology industry to discuss the concept he had in mind. He was all doing this amidst his illness.

Initially, the Apple team was thinking of how to make the iPod evolve into a smartphone. During this time, they were also secretly brainstorming about their plans eventually to come up with a tablet computer – which later on became popularly known as the iPad. This brainstorming ultimately led to the iPhone concept. In other words, the iPad idea came before the advent of the iPhone.

Jony Ive presented to Steve the touchscreen feature for the Apple tablet, which was, fortunately, approved by Steve. Steve then thought of incorporating such feature in the iPhone.

Steve's obsession for perfectionism and control over everything was reflected on the features of the iPhone. The iPhone was intentionally made to be tightly sealed and even the user would not be able to open it. Unlike with other smartphones, the user would not be able to open the iPhone to change the battery. In fact, a broken iPhone could not be brought to any generic service center as it could not be easily opened using commercially available screwdrivers or other tools.

In January 2007, the very first iPhone was launched at Macworld in San Francisco. Steve invited the former Apple executives and the original Macintosh division.

The iPhone was considered to be the most expensive phone worldwide. Nonetheless, approximately ninety million units were sold in a span of three years.

CHAPTER THIRTY-SEVEN

ROUND TWO

The Cancer Recurs

In 2008, Steve's cancer was spreading and his obsession with restrictive fasts and diets – which he learned as a young adult in the middle of his spiritual journey – was not helping him recover. This apparently resulted in severe weight loss. His wife Laurene even hired a great cook but even the most sumptuous dishes did not address Steve's eating disorder at all.

During the launching of the iPhone 3G, Steve was so thin that his product announcement was overshadowed by his physical appearance. When his weight loss became a public issue, Apple released a statement indicating that Steve's health condition was a private matter.

Steve began cancelling interviews, meetings, and events one after another because of his health situation. He even had to cancel his appearance at the Macworld forum that was to be held in January 2009. He subsequently released a public statement that his absence was because of hormonal imbalance and because he wanted more time with his family.

Soon thereafter, he informed Apple officers and staff that he would be on medical leave and that the daily operations at Apple would again be monitored by Tim Cook.

During this time, he badly needed a liver transplant, which was successfully done in March 2009 at Memphis, Tennessee. During the operation, the doctors suspected that the cancer could have migrated elsewhere. Some, including his family, even thought that he might not be able to make it after the operation. Nevertheless, Steve did.

From Memphis, he and his family flew back to Palo Alto in May 2009 and even attended a board meeting that was held a few days after his return. In June, he was conducting meetings with Apple officers and staff on a daily basis. In July, he was back on his feet and started coming to work on a daily basis.

CHAPTER THIRTY-EIGHT

THE iPAD

Into the Post-PC Era

In January 2010, Jobs unveiled the very first iPad in San Francisco, California. Again, he made sure that he invited the original members of the Apple team. However, this time, his surgeons Jeffrey Norton and James Eason were part of the audience.

Before the iPad went on sale, Steve and the entire Apple team were getting criticisms. Some said that the iPad was like an iPhone on steroids, or why was there no USB cord, and so on and so forth. These complaints actually depressed Steve as he worried about its marketability.

The iPad went on sale in April 2010 and before the month even ended, Apple already sold approximately one million iPads – even surpassing, by some measures, the sale performance of the iPhone.

The mobile applications found in the iPad were also those found in the iPhone. These apps were exclusively available in Apple products only and could not be accessed by Android users. Steve was adamant about it as he did not want Apple users to infect their gadgets with viruses. He did not want outsiders to pollute the integrity of the features of the Apple products. However, in the long run, Steve also approved outsiders to develop apps for Apple but with conditions.

The digital world indeed had a fundamental transportation with the emergence of both the iTunes Store and the App Store, which had both been successfully released by Apple.

CHAPTER THIRTY-NINE

NEW BATTLES

And Echoes of Old Ones

The decision of Google to introduce the Android operating system infuriated Steve mainly because he felt betrayed – Google CEO Eric Schmidt formed part of Apple's board of directors. Apple refused to enter the search business to prevent them from competing against Google. Nonetheless, Google ventured into the phone business. To make matters worse, Google eventually introduced smartphones with touchscreen features.

Aside from Google, Steve was also in a legal battle against Adobe during this time, but the conflict between the two could be traced as far back as 1985, when Adobe refused to develop software for Apple. However, Steve still believed that all conflicts could be resolved through compromise, and that was how Apple and Adobe resolved their issues. Steve lifted some of Apple's restrictions to allow Adobe to develop a compatible tool for Apple's iOS.

During this time, Apple also discovered a flaw in their iPhone 4 product. This led Steve to hold meetings 24/7 with different key players in Apple and other companies. He also made sure to bring along his son Reed to every meeting he attended. He emphasized to Reed that attending meetings with him would help him learn a lot about business.

Apparently, with Steve's health condition, he simply wanted to expose his son to his world before it was too late.

CHAPTER FORTY

TO INFINITY

The Cloud, the Spaceship, and Beyond

Steve thought that he would not be able to attend the launching of the iPad 2 because he was once again on medical leave. Nonetheless, on March 2, 2011, Steve was there to present the new gadget. He was thin and pale but, on the other hand, he was wearing a carefree smile – he was obviously excited to introduce the iPad 2. His unwavering enthusiasm, despite his sickness, earned him a standing ovation.

During this time, Steve was busy monitoring the progress of the creation of three Pixar films, namely, "Toy Story 3," "The Bourne Ultimatum," and "Chinatown." He was also busy preparing a surprise for his wife Laurene for their twentieth wedding anniversary. He was also busy designing and building a yacht with the help of yacht manufacturer Feadship. Steve was, of course, not sure about how long – or short – he would live but dreaming and planning about the yacht gave him hope that he might still live for a few more years.

In 2011, Steve also made sure that the features of the iCloud were strengthened. It was in 2008 when Steve envisioned the use of "the cloud." He wanted Apple users to stop using their Apple gadgets to store content, they should use cloud storage instead.

The iCloud was formally launched at the Worldwide Developers Conference in June 2011. On the following day, he unveiled his plans to construct a building that would become Apple's signature campus.

CHAPTER FORTY-ONE

ROUND THREE

The Twilight Struggle

In 2009, Steve's son Reed seemed to have matured fast. All of a sudden, he started looking after his sisters especially when their parents were away. However, when Steve's health condition improved in 2010, Reed sort of loosened up and got back to his cheerful personality.

In one of the school competitions that Reed participated in, all contestants were asked what their ambition was. Without any hesitation, Reed said that he wanted to be a cancer researcher.

Steve always wished and prayed to have the energy to attend the important events in Reed's life, most especially his graduation. That's why Steve was extremely happy to have attended Reed's high school graduation ceremony.

Steve and Reed apparently had a very close father-and-son relationship. Nevertheless, Steve was somewhat distant to his other children. In spite of the fact that the daughters were treated differently, they had all learned how to deal with their father's behavior and they grew up to be good children. Besides, Steve was never a bad father to them, anyway. In fact, in 2010, when Jobs' health somewhat improved, he took his whole family to Japan.

In 2011, Steve was on his third medical leave. Even before his doctors detected it, he already knew that his cancer reappeared because he started losing his appetite and he was always in horrendous pain. Unlike Steve's previous medical leaves, the third one prompted several people to visit him. Among them were Google co-founder Larry Page, U.S. President Bill Clinton, and Bill Gates.

On August 24, 2011, Steve attended a board meeting to announce his resignation and that Tim Cook will be taking his place as CEO of Apple.

CHAPTER FORTY-TWO

LEGACY

The Brightest Heave of Invention

Steve had always wanted to establish a company where people would exceedingly be inspired to create stellar products. Creating great products was his top priority; generating profit and everything else were only secondary.

Steve did not believe that businesses should provide whatever the customers want. For him, businesses should introduce products to customers and make them realize that they need those products.

Months before his death, Steve was grateful to have witnessed that Apple had indeed surpassed the sales performance of Microsoft in terms of being the most valuable technology company worldwide.

Indeed, Steve's and Apple's remarkable success resulted from his obsession from control, focus, artistry, desires, perfectionism, and passion, among many others.

Steve Jobs died on October 5, 2011. Indeed, he had a life well lived.

Conclusion

This book narrates Steve Jobs' inspiring and audacious life from the time that he was born until the time of his death.

This book is highly recommended to all, more particularly to:

- anyone curious about the life of Steve Jobs;

- anyone curious about the massive success achieved by Apple;

- anyone curious about how the Apple gadgets we use now came to be;

- entrepreneurs and businessmen;

- executives;

- employees, specifically those who don't understand why their employers are harsh at times;

- students;

- anyone who needs to be motivated in life;

- anyone who wants to know how perseverance, determination, and grit could lead to success.

Final Thoughts

Hey! Did you enjoy this book? We sincerely hope you thoroughly enjoyed this short read and have gotten immensely valuable insights that will help you in any areas of your life.

Would it be too greedy if we ask for a review from you?

It takes 1 minute to leave 1 review to possibly influence 1 more person's decision to read just 1 book which may change their 1 life. Your 1 minute matters and we value it and thank you so much for giving us your 1 minute. If it sucks, just say it sucks. Period.

FREE BONUS

P.S. Is it okay if we overdeliver?

Here at Abbey Beathan Publishing, we believe in overdelivering way beyond our reader's expectations. Is it okay if we overdeliver?

Here's the deal, we're going to give you an extremely valuable cheatsheet of "Accelerated Learning". We've partnered up with Ikigai Publishing to present to you the exclusive bonus of "Accelerated Learning Cheatsheet"

What's the catch? We need to trust you... You see, we want to overdeliver and in order for us to do that, we've to trust our reader to keep this bonus a secret to themselves. Why? Because we don't want people to be getting our exclusive accelerated learning cheatsheet without even buying our books itself. Unethical, right?

Ok. Are you ready?

Simply Visit this link: http://bit.ly/acceleratedcheatsheet

We hope you'll enjoy our free bonuses as much as we've enjoyed preparing it for you!

Free Bonus #2: Free Book Preview of Summary: Love & Respect

The Book at a Glance

This book is about how both the husband and the wife can appreciate, respect, and understand each other.

This book has three parts. The first part is about the crazy cycle – why husbands do not love their wife and why their wives won't respect their husband. The second part of this book is about the energizing cycle – how husbands can love their wife and how wives can respect their husband. The third part is about the rewarded cycle – the real reason why both men and women should love and respect their spouses.

Chapter 1 – This talks about how love alone is not enough to make a marriage work. The simple secret to a happy marriage is respect.

Chapter 2 – Men and women hear and see things differently. This chapter talks about the coded message that men and women send to each other.

Chapter 3 – In this chapter, you'll learn why women do not respect their husbands and why husbands do not love their wives.

Chapter 4 – This chapter talks about why husband stonewall their wives.

Chapter 5 – In chapter 5, you'll learn how to break the cycle. Respecting your husband does not mean that you have to be a doormat.

Chapter 6 – This chapter encourages spouses to be mature enough to make the first move.

Chapter 7 – This chapter is about respect and how it can motivate a man to love his wife.

Chapter 8 – This chapter is about the acronym COUPLE (closeness, openness, understanding, peacemaking, loyalty, and esteem).

Chapter 9 – This chapter talks about how important closeness is to women.

Chapter 10 – This is about how a husband can open up to his wife.

Chapter 11 – This chapter talks about how a husband can show his wife that he understands him.

Chapter 12 – This chapter is about the power of "I'm sorry".

Chapter 13 – This chapter is about how important loyalty is to women.

Chapter 14 – This is about how man can respect and honor his wife.

Chapter 15 – This chapter talks about how wives can get into the energizing cycle by understanding the acronym CHAIRS (Conquest, Hierarchy, Authority, Insight, Relationship, and Sexuality).

Chapter 16 – This talks about how a man values his work and how a woman can respect him by appreciating what he brings to the table.

Chapter 17 – This chapter is about the man's need to provide and protect his family. A wife should not belittle her husband's work.

Chapter 18 – This chapter talks about the husband's need to lead his family.

Chapter 19 – A woman must appreciate his desire to give advice to his wife.

Chapter 20 – This chapter is about the man's need to have a "shoulder to shoulder."

Chapter 21 – This chapter is about how important physical intimacy is to a husband.

Chapter 22 – This summarizes how both the husband and wife can get into the energizing cycle.

Chapter 23 – This is about the real reason why spouses should love and respect one another.

Chapter 24 – This chapter talks about the real reward of unconditional love and respect.

This book will help you cherish, value, and appreciate your spouse. What you are about to read is powerful enough to save your marriage.

Introduction: Love Alone Is Not Enough

Do you want to be closer to your spouse? Do you want to achieve harmony in the household? Do you want to feel understood? Do you want to have a blissful marriage that's free of needless pain? Then, read this book.

The Beatles sang, "All you need is love." Well, that's not true at all.

Half of marriages end in divorce because love is simply not enough to keep a marriage going. Love is important, especially for women. However, what we all miss is the husband's need for respect. This book is about how the wife can fulfill her need to be loved by giving her husband the one thing that he needs – respect.

This book contains vital information that will help you save your marriage and build a deep relationship with your spouse. This book is for those who are going through marital problems. It is also for people who want to stay happily married until death. It is also for jaded divorcees, lonely wives, spouses who have been cheated on, and engage couples. It is also for counselors and pastors who want to save marriages.

This book contains information that's powerful enough to

bring spouses closer to each other. However, what you are about to read is not a "miracle pill". Sometimes, the glow a spouse feels after reading this book fades in just a few weeks. They go back to the "crazy" cycle. You must practice the tips contained in this book for at least six weeks. This will help you make "respect" a part of your system. The quest for a happy and satisfying marriage is an ongoing process. It's never over.

If you're struggling with marriage, you should know that respect might be the missing piece of the puzzle. Read on to discover the power of respect.

Part One: The Crazy Cycle

He reacts to her without love

She reacts to him without respect

The major problem of the wives is that they feel that their husband do not love them. You see, wives are made to expect, want, and make love. And many husbands fail to meet this vital need. After studying the scriptures and various books, Dr. Emerson Eggerichs found the other half of the equation.

Husbands do not complain much. Nevertheless, most of them have one concern – their wives do not respect them. This is the reason why fifty percent of marriages end in divorce. When a wife feels that her husband doesn't love her, she disrespects him. When a husband doesn't get respect from his wife, he acts without love. This cycle goes round and round. This is called the "crazy cycle". The first seven chapters of this book talks about the "crazy cycle" – what is it and how you can get out of it.

Read More...

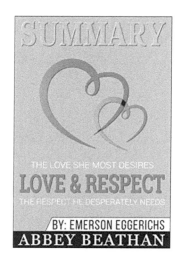

CPSIA information can be obtained
at www.ICGtesting.com
Printed in the USA
BVHW070948190619
551408BV00005B/398/P

9 781646 153572